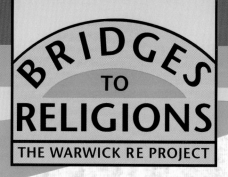

BRIDGES TO RELIGIONS
THE WARWICK RE PROJECT

The Buddha's Birthday

Written by Margaret Barratt

Series editors: Judith Everington
and Robert Jackson

Acknowledgements

Thanks are due to Aung's family; the Ven. Ajahn Khemadhammo; and Joyce Miller.

Thanks are due to the following for the use of the original photographs: Noel Barratt, Back cover, p.1, 4, 6–10, 12–15, 17–22; Hilary Roberts, 5, 6, 16; Peter Roberts, Front cover, 11, 23.

98 97 96 95
10 9 8 7 6 5 4 3 2

British Cataloguing in Publication Data
A catalogue record for this book is available from the British Library

ISBN 0 435 30407 0 (One each of 5 titles)
ISBN 0 435 30406 2 (5 x The Buddha's Birthday, Paperback)
ISBN 0 431 07734 7 (The Buddha's Birthday, Hardback)

Heinemann Educational Publishers,
A Division of Heinemann Publishers (Oxford) Ltd,
Halley Court, Jordan Hill, Oxford OX2 8EJ

OXFORD LONDON EDINBURGH
MADRID ATHENS BOLOGNA PARIS
MELBOURNE SYDNEY AUCKLAND SINGAPORE
TOKYO IBADAN NAIROBI HARARE
GABORONE PORTSMOUTH NH (USA)

Designed and typeset by Green Door Design Ltd
Printed in Hong Kong

Contents

Special Words

Ajahn (Pronounced <u>Ah</u>-jan)
  The senior monk

Buddha (Pronounced <u>Bud</u>-da)
  A very important teacher

Buddhist (Pronounced <u>Bud</u>-ist)
  A follower of the Buddha

Stupa (Pronounced <u>stoo</u>-pa)
  A pointed tower

Wesak (Pronounced <u>weh</u>-sack)
  A festival on the Buddha's Birthday

Aung is a Buddhist boy.

He visits the monks at the monastery.

He hopes he will make new friends there.

The monks have shaved heads and
wear long robes.

It is the Buddha's birthday today.

The day is called Wesak.

Aung will remember the Buddha.

He was an important teacher.

He taught people how to be happy.

Aung leaves his shoes outside the shrine room.

He walks quietly inside.

The beautiful statues of the Buddha help people to remember him.

There are candles near the statues.

There are flowers in vases.

Aung's uncle lights incense sticks.

It is so peaceful here.

The senior monk is called the Ajahn.
The Ajahn chants important words.
People put their hands together
and join in the chant.
They promise to live good lives.

There is a beautiful feast.
Everyone has brought some food.
Most of it is made from plants.
The Buddha said it is wrong
to hurt living creatures.

Everyone holds a bowl of food.

The monks come with empty bowls.

Aung puts some food into their bowls.

The monks look into the bowl, not at
the food or at the people.
They don't choose what to have.
The people give the monks food to
say thank you for teaching them.

Wesak is a special day so
the monks' bowls are very full.
Aung sees Arjuna in the circle.
Aung wants to be friends but
Arjuna is very shy.

Now everyone fills their plates to take outside for a picnic.
They talk to old friends and make new ones.

Aung sees the Buddha statue by
the pool.
Aung likes to look for creatures in
the water.

It is time to remember the Buddha.
Aung lights his candle.
Everyone joins in a long line.

The Ajahn holds a lotus flower.
He leads everyone around a
tower called a stupa.
They all think about the Buddha and
say his name to themselves.

They walk round again.
This time they think about
what the Buddha taught people.
On the third walk round they think
about all the monks and nuns.

Aung gently places his candle with
the incense sticks and flowers.
He bows to show respect for
the Buddha.

The grown-ups go indoors to
listen to the Ajahn.
Aung and his new friends hear a
story about how to be happy.

The children make some cards to wish the monks a happy Wesak.

The children take their cards inside to
give them to the monks.
The Ajahn is pleased.
He gives each child some sweets.
He tells them, "Be well and happy."

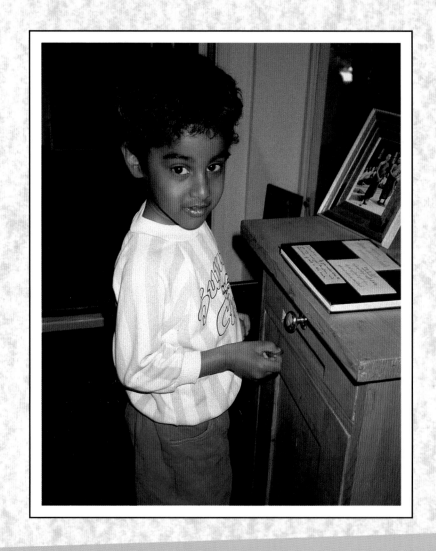

Arjuna is giving a present too.
He puts some money in the box to
help look after the monastery.

Everyone has had a happy day.
They had fun but they also
remembered the Buddha.
They were thankful that he came
to teach people how to be happy.

Index